12984/1

# Airline Pilot

## by Leonie Bennett

**Editorial consultant: Mitch Cronick**

Copyright © **ticktock Entertainment Ltd 2006**

First published in Great Britain in 2006 by **ticktock Media Ltd.,**

Unit 2, Orchard Business Centre, North Farm Road, Tunbridge Wells, Kent TN2 3XF

**We would like to thank: Shirley Bickler and Suzanne Baker**

ISBN 1 86007 995 4 pbk

Printed in China

Picture credits

t=top, b=bottom, c=centre, l-left, r=right, OFC= outside front cover

AirTeamImages (Tomas Coelho): 15. BAA Aviation Photo Library: 11.
Cameron Bowerman: 20-21. Corbis: 4. The Flight Collection: 9, 10, 16, 17, 21t.
Brian Futterman: 19. Daniel Hamer: 12. John Kelly: 6–7.
Gary Lewis (ATCO Aviation photography): 13.

Every effort has been made to trace the copyright holders, and we apologise in advance for any
unintentional omissions. We would be pleased to insert the appropriate acknowledgements in any
subsequent edition of this publication.

# CONTENTS

# Mike the pilot

My name is Mike.

I'm an airline pilot.

Today I am going to fly from London to New York.

London is in England.

New York is in America.

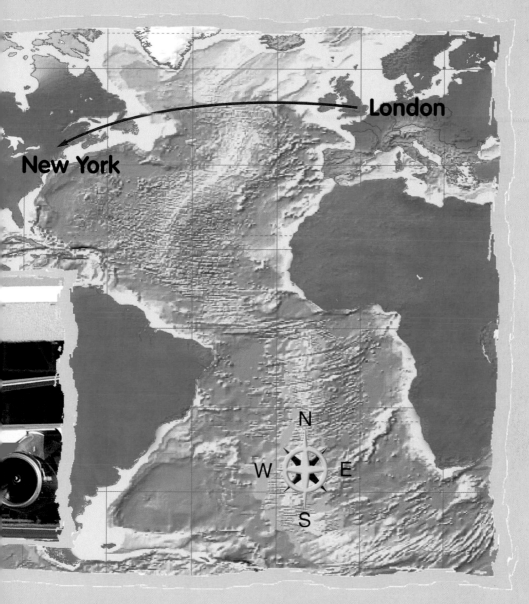

It takes six hours to fly from
London to New York.

# Let's look at the plane

I am going to fly this jumbo jet.

A jumbo jet is one of the biggest planes in the world.

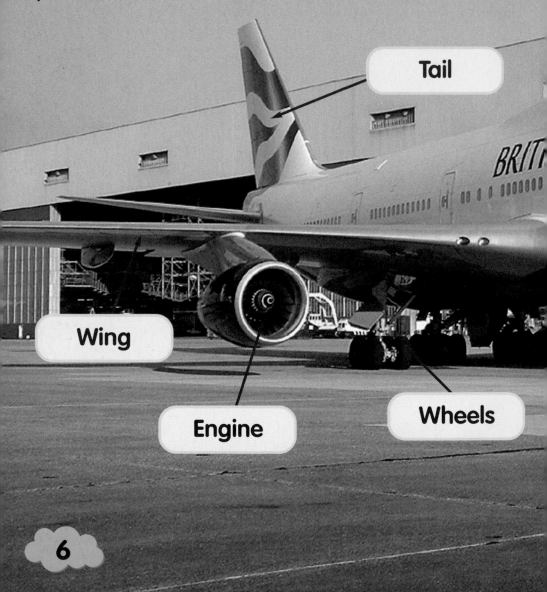

Tail

Wing

Engine

Wheels

A jumbo jet has 188 windows and 18 wheels.

Cockpit

Windows

Door

I sit at the front, in the cockpit.

# Checking the plane

I get to the airport early because there are lots of jobs to do.

First I must check the outside of the plane.

I check the wheels.

I check the lights.

I look in the engines.

It is important that everything is working.

Wheels

# In the cockpit

I am the captain and Don is the co-pilot.

He will help me fly the plane.

There are lots of controls in the cockpit.

I check that they are all working before we take off.

Controls

Then I check the weather forecast.

| Sunny | Rainy | Stormy | Snowy |

Don checks the map.

**Map**

# Take-off

We have done all our checks.

Everything is OK.

We are ready for take-off so we start the engines.

Runway

The plane moves down the runway very fast. It goes faster and faster.

Then it takes off into the sky.

**Wheels**

When the plane is up in the air, the wheels fold up into the plane.

# Flying to America

There are 412 passengers on this plane.

The passengers are reading or sleeping.

Soon the flight attendants will give them food and drinks.

Some of the passengers are watching a film.

**Flight attendant**

# Pilots at work

Don and I are working.

Don checks the weather. Then he checks the fuel.

I check what speed the plane is going. We are flying at 570 miles per hour

**In-flight meal**

The flight attendant brings us food and drinks in the cockpit.

# Landing

We are getting near to New York.

I ask air traffic control if
we can land.

**Air traffic control**

They check the weather is OK.

They check that there are no
other planes on the runway.

They say that I can land the plane.

The wheels unfold ready for landing.

# Welcome to New York

As the plane lands, it is still going about 150 miles per hour.

When the plane has stopped, the passengers get off.

Runway

We are in New York!

It was a good flight and everyone is happy.

Passengers

Wheels

# Thinking and talking about pilots

What do the
pilots do before
take-off?

How many
wheels does a
jumbo jet have?

Why do you think there are two pilots?

What would be the best thing about being an airline pilot?

What do you think would be the worst thing about being an airline pilot?

# Activities

What did you think of this book?

What was the most interesting fact you found in this book?

• • • • • • • • • • • • • •

Which is the odd one out? Why?

**engines • lights • map • wheels**

• • • • • • • • • • • • • •

Draw a big picture of a jumbo jet and label it. Use these words:

**cockpit • door • engine • wheels • window • wing**

• • • • • • • • • • • • •

Who is the author of this book?
Have you read *Animal Hospital* by the same author?